About the Author

Aya, Author, Poet, Politician, Philosopher, and Educator.

Pocket Philosophy

Aya G. K

Pocket Philosophy

Olympia Publishers
London

www.olympiapublishers.com
OLYMPIA PAPERBACK EDITION

Copyright © Aya G. K 2024

The right of Aya G. K to be identified as author of
this work has been asserted in accordance with sections 77 and 78 of
the Copyright, Designs and Patents Act 1988.

All Rights Reserved

No reproduction, copy or transmission of this publication
may be made without written permission.
No paragraph of this publication may be reproduced,
copied or transmitted save with the written permission of the publisher,
or in accordance with the provisions
of the Copyright Act 1956 (as amended).

Any person who commits any unauthorised act in relation to
this publication may be liable to criminal
prosecution and civil claims for damage.

A CIP catalogue record for this title is
available from the British Library.

ISBN: 978-1-80439-613-1

This is a work of fiction.
Names, characters, places and incidents originate from the writer's
imagination. Any resemblance to actual persons, living or dead, is
purely coincidental.

First Published in 2024

Olympia Publishers
Tallis House
2 Tallis Street
London
EC4Y 0AB

Printed in Great Britain

Acknowledgements

This is an acknowledgment of the outstanding people I have in my life, who drenched me in love in support.
This is also an acknowledgment of the exceptional characters, my mentors, whom I was lucky enough to encounter, you taught me a lot.
Thank you for your contribution in this Journey, and beyond it.
All the love, always!

Letter to Loved Ones

This one goes out to my family, friends, mentors and loved ones. The people who shape every ounce of my existence. The people who make anything and everything worth it by being part of it. The people who fill my life with love, light and knowledge.
This book is <u>about you</u>, <u>for you</u> and <u>by you</u>. So, thank you for this, and for everything.
    Love you now, later, and forever,
    Aya.

Playlist

I believe that this book is an experience, and that I would like to share this experience with you, so you can live the whole experience with me.

So, here is a list of songs I listened to while I wrote. Enjoy.

1- 'Enta Omry' — By Om Kalthoum.
2- Purple Rain — By Prince.
3- Summertime Sadness — By Lana Del Rey.
4- That's Amore — By Dean Martin.
5- 'Batwanes Beik' — By Warda.
6- Breakdown Mode — By Iyeoka.
7- Earned It — By the Weeknd.
8- I'd do anything for love — By Meatloaf & Cher.
9- Heartless — By Kanye West.
10- Alone — By Burna Boy.
11- Starboy — By the Weeknd.
12- Love — By Kendrick Lamar.
13- I Will Always Love You — By Dolly Parton.
14- The Godfather — By Guns n Roses.
15- Girls Got Rhythm — By AC/DC.
16- The Thrill is Gone — By BB King.
17- Higher — By Rihanna.
18- Pills n Potions — By Nicki Minaj.
19- Kiss of Life — By Sade.
20- Trillions — By Alicia Keys & Brent Faiyz.
21- Snooze -By SZA.
22- Best Part- Daniel Caesar & H.E.R
23- 'Keifak Enta'-Fairouz.

Author's Note

Ancient Greek philosophy has been one of my fascinations since I was in high school. From Socrates to Aristotle, I always enjoyed and appreciated their inquiry and curiosity, and I am very thankful for all the enlightenment they brought to the world. Since then, life for me became all about observing, analyzing, and asking questions. I look for deeper meanings and understandings of the world, channeling myself into discussions that grow to become ideas and questions.

Yet everything I synthesize I synthesize through my own personal experience. Like the legendary, one-of-a-kind Frida Kahlo once said, "I paint myself because I am often alone and I am the subject I know best", and as I write I feel this notion. Because what I project through my writing is ideas and questions but through me, and this is what I love about every piece, that it may be through me, yet it opens a door for different interpretations according to every single person who reads it. Creating a brand-new perspective or widening another.

However, as personal as it gets, I am a great fan of diversity; simply I adore it, for me it's food for my curious mind. Therefore, every piece I write or will write could be tailored to every one's unique personal experience. So, I hope with every piece you read it becomes a compass for your own unique identified soul.

At the end, speaking frankly from my heart to yours, I wish I can have a conversation with each one before and after reading this book, before and after I shared a part of me with every one of you.

Love, Freedom and Dinner

I sit around and wonder about how much we have said in the unsaid. I say one thing and I mean another, or how everything we think is always concealed, like I get that, but I don't really like it. So as the human I am, I love asking people about their feelings, ask the uncomfortable questions and watch them stutter, like I walked in on them in the bathroom. So, this time (by accident to be brutally honest) I took a different approach, but aren't accidents really fate with a mask, that gets us where we should be?

Getting back to the point I went around asking a few silly questions, this, and that, just to talk and discuss. Then, boom! Oh my god how heated things turned out, and how awesome these discussions were. There were simple meanings that had more to them, stuff that made me remember things I've read before, and stuff that made me learn a thing or two about having perspective.

Before I dive into how things turned out, I'll give you the questions I went around asking. Answer them, and then I'll tell you all about everyone else.

1- The famous most generic: if you could have dinner with anyone in the world: dead or alive, real or fake who would they be? And why?

2- In one word what does love mean for you?

3- What is your definition of freedom?

So, the questions seem fine right, basic. Yet asking around for a bit I got a tiny bit of insight on what people want most, what they lack, who they are and what they conceal in the backs of their heads. An interesting part was how much was said out loud replying to these questions under "joking", and as much as I love to joke, I know how much truth we have in it, believe me I do.

Maybe that's why Plato didn't like it. Plato believed that laughter and mockery are part of superiority, as by making a joke about someone we believe ourselves to be superior to them. Maybe that explain when we mock our own ideas and truths that we believe should not be clearly out there. To become superior to ideas we think are unfitting or wrong, because only we have superiority we have full power of disclosure, we have authority on such ideas.

However, beyond Plato's Superiority, humor and sarcasm are also used to mask the things we are unable to say or communicate clearly. The things that would be unacceptable said out loud, or to the public, therefore the sarcasm and mockery. Enabling us to say what is not usually said, because at the end of the day it's just a 'Joke'.

Like for me

A friend can be like: "Why aren't you coming out today?"

Me: *in my most sarcastic tone ever* "Because I don't feel like seeing you guys. Duh."

A friend: *laughing hysterically* "No really, please come."

Me: *laughing hysterically* (making up an excuse) "No really, I have to see my parents today."

So, no offense intended I didn't feel like hanging out with them, and my sarcastic tone made it even better because I don't have to lie about it either. This is kinda close to one thing that happened when I went around asking those questions.

One case was thirty-seven-year-old women with three kids.

Me: "I'll ask you a question about life."

Her: "Yeah that'll be fun!"

Me: *gets comfy in my seat and then shoots* "Okay! So, tell me, what is your definition of freedom?"

Then she looks at her kids, laughs mockingly, turns to me, and in the same sarcastic tone I use on my friends she says, "life without kids" and laughs.

To be honest I laugh back, but it rings.

Then she switches back quickly and says, "No, for real, freedom is when I was able to take my decisions free of chains, and without thinking a lot." She pauses for a quick moment and says, "Actually not thinking at all." And laughs again.

I honestly laughed back, said, "Ohhhh myyy goooddd yess, but a little utopian freedom don't you think?" Then cracked a few jokes and moved on.

Yet, this is the same thing I do over and over with my friends, and a few other things, so in a way I get the 'sarcasm'.

The idea is that it's not that I don't love my friends; I do, I deeply do. I just don't feel like seeing them from time to time. Like this woman loves her kids and if the time went back, she'd have them all over again, but from time to time she feels burdened. I am not judging her by any means like the wise Samantha Jones once said, "It's not my style!" Three kids and a job like I can't imagine the last time she took a carefree decision.

Yet, "by accident" the moment I asked the question was a time of distress for her, and a simple question like that just made me know something she'd never confess out loud cause if she did, she'd be tabooed for life.

Without digging too deep into this, it's just disappointing how a society like ours would throw away the awesome mom she is and how she's the arms, eyes and feet of three children, and would condemn her for voicing an emotion.

And just like that! One simple question hid fear, shame, and mixed feelings under a fake laugh and a sarcastic tone.

Moving from this specific answer. Discussing freedom with many people was many things. Maybe what they needed at the moment, or maybe just an outtake on this and that. But just sitting back and listening, I saw what some needed, how some thought about things. The less I spoke, and the more I opened my ears (which I dread), I realized things I never knew I needed to realize, and realized how many things I thought were important that don't really matter as much.

So enough on freedom let's dive into love. Love is a concept that is amazingly narrowed down in my perspective, and because of this (even if it's a little unfair) I decided to narrow down the description to one word. It's amazing because, think about it, love is everywhere around us and relates to many things, so this was actually a way to see how people would describe "many things" in one short word (no pressure intended thoo).

Let me give you my answer in a simple yet more personal note, I love bubble tea. So, I drive twenty-two kilometers in total every one or two days to go get bubble tea from the place I like. So, unconsciously, when I ask myself this question "what is love?" I quickly reply with 'love is passion', and then I think about it for a moment, and it makes sense, right? Because I am the type of person who "loves" bubble tea and drives twenty-two kilometers nearly daily just to go get some, it makes sense that I'd say love is passion. Because only a passionate feeling would drive me to drive forty minutes regularly for something I "love".

Three other people I asked this question to, in an alarmingly quick time span (compared to everyone I asked), said comfort. Love is comfort. Then I thought about those three, their life, their relationships, like in general, thinking to myself, "Hey. To have the same answer that quickly to the same question, what the hell could they have in common?"

They are very different people to be brutally honest, like age wise, life wise, relationship wise, and even mindset wise, it was like looking for a needle in a pile of hay! But then I came across some significant aspects that were right under my nose. Aspects like how they love staying at home, how each one of them has a few foods they "love" that they practically don't change, and how they hardly make any new friends (regardless of how different their time at home is, how different these foods are, and how different each one of their friend groups are).

Then I have an epiphany and then comfort just came in like a blizzard, and as much as this is a horror movie for a person like me who hardly eats something they've had two weeks ago because they'd get bored as hell! It did explain "comfort". They don't love comfort, love for them is what gives them comfort, love is whatever brings it, it's wherever there is comfort there is love, and whatever love is, it must be comfortable.

The last book I read was Gibran Khalil Gibran's *The Prophet*. Regardless of how much I loved his unrealistic, utopian concepts of life and love, he had one concept that struck me. The concept was on love and autonomy, he said that two people in love are like two different harps but playing the same note. That is one of the most beautiful concepts I've read when it comes to love and relationships, it rang, but what made it live a little inside my head, was one of the definitions of love I heard.

When I asked one of the most driven, independent and established people I know "What is love in one word?" their answer was "SHARING", which for me was crazy because to be honest I expected something more like 'power' for example. Because in my head I thought of this person in the context of "you need no one, you got this", so it put me in a "???!!!??!!" moment.

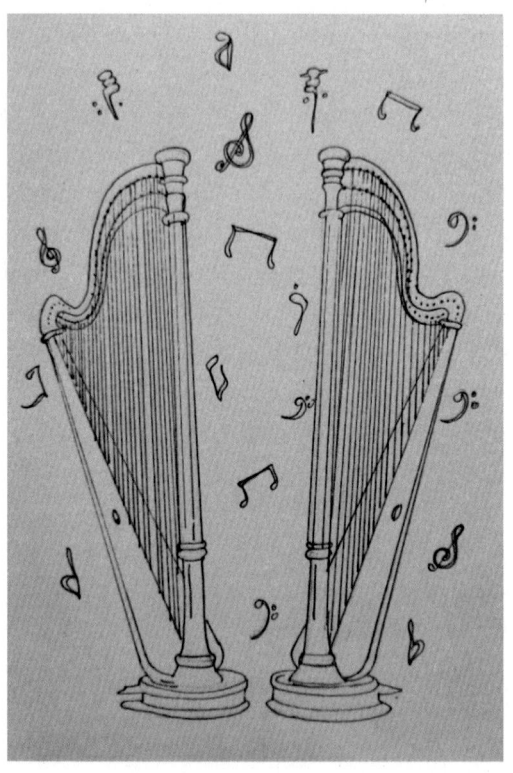

Then at this moment I remembered Gibran, and thought of this person as a harp, and it's playing this amazing note, right. Then I pictured how beautiful this note would be if another harp played it as well, and how both harps would feel if they knew they were playing the same note together. In one sense the note would be louder, stronger, and more beautiful for everyone listening to it. Yet, I think about the harp itself, and how it would feel.

Maybe it would feel safer, more confident, and at ease, knowing that even though the note is beautiful, it's not playing it alone, and there is another harp that gets it and is playing it too. Then I think to myself, yes, this IS a way to explain love. It's not

NEEDING someone to play so the note would get out, but autonomously playing the note, and knowing that there is someone else that is sharing this same note with you.

Then there were lots of other things. Like love is unconditional, love is reciprocation, love is real, and love is safety. So, whatever we see as love I really hope we never settle for anything that doesn't provide us with it.

Then life takes me to a beach trip with my friends and then the clock strikes ten p.m. and while we are chilling together, joking around, and having a good time I decide to pause for a moment, and ask them.

"Okay, I want each one of you to tell me someone dead, alive, fiction, or real you would want to have dinner with and why?"

They gave me a hard time for a bit and told me that I need to give them a break from my questions. But I didn't care, because they're my friends and they literally signed up for this, so I demanded answers anyways. And because I am a bossy friend they gave up and started thinking of who. So, after a few minutes' answers began flowing in.

Some of them had questions for people who were long dead, so they decided to use their dinners to meet those people and ask those questions. Others were more interested in living icons of inventions and success like Elon Musk, which is very fair because like ELON MUSK! Who doesn't want to have dinner with Elon Musk? Some had answers ready and set in stone, others bounced names of people around because they thought they're awesome in some way or another.

It was a round discussion, answers flew in, we talked, they

justified, we discussed, it was nice (and time consuming to be honest).

Yet at the end of the day this question specifically is very personal, and each answer is based on nothing but personal preference and mindset, so each answer was fair and interesting based on the person saying it.

Even for me it was extremely personal. In a heartbeat I said Socrates, because obviously you can tell I like analyzing, finding philosophy in things, and asking the questions, like my eyes would literally light up every time anyone brought up Socrates or the Socratic Method. And Socrates to be honest is the father of all this crap, he died for it for god's sake, and what is more committed than that? So, when it came down to this question specifically it's just a matter of persona.

Just one specific friend of mine didn't answer that night, then got lost amidst all the debating and discussing, but who were they fooling? I let it slide but not for long.

Then one week goes by and I ask this same friend this same question again, and they still have no answer. So, we spent thirty minutes discussing (hoping I'd get an answer) and still no solid answer.

Then like two more weeks go by and I ask again and still NO ANSWER. My friend justifies this no answer curse and tells me that they thought about it and they're taking the question seriously, but it's just that no one pops in their head. At this point, I snapped. Like three weeks are more than enough. So, I said what J Cole once said: "Fool me one time shame you, fool me two times shame on me, fool me three times f the peace sign," so I decided I won't be fooled the third time and pinned them down, and at this point they answered.

For me I chose Socrates, but I have an infinite list of people I would love to have dinner with, painters, musicians, leaders, entrepreneurs, and many others. Lots of great minds, things I'd love to know and discuss and people I would love to meet. So how could someone not have anyone in their head for three weeks right? Then I thought about it for a bit, and it all became explanatory all at once, like a blizzard.

First, not everyone is me, which sucks.

Second, I couldn't not appreciate this friend. This is a mythological question, like if they decided to say anyone it's fine, but the premeditation and self-accountability were astonishing for me.

I know I am using big words, but to break them down. Premeditation is knowing something very well beforehand. In this case it resembled an awesome indication of knowing what an opportunity really means, even mythologically, like one person, one dinner, even if not for real, is an opportunity. Therefore, it must be someone they are sure of, someone that IS the person they'd use their opportunity on. Which is a level of knowing something's worth regardless of if it's real or not.

Then I thought to myself, if this was really going to happen will Socrates really be it for me? or did I just say that because it's not really happening and it makes sense for me, so why not? Life is simpler than that, I get it, but even risks are better calculated, and this friend of mine made my impulsive side take a bow.

The self-accountability was like a charm on me as well. The fact that this person knew that they're answering this question in-front of themselves before anybody else, made me stop and clap. Because a big piece of most of the people just wanted to get their answers out on the table, tell everyone about them. Yet when it came to this one specifically, they wanted to get the answer out to themselves, then out to everyone. So, it took time to formulate the answer they'd be accountable for, before hearing anyone else's response.

At the end of the day, I did pressure this friend of mine to get the answer out of them, because for me no opportunity lasts forever (certainly not three long weeeeeekkksss), and to be honest I got curious, so I had to physically pin them down.

Besides curiosity, leaving opportunities hanging out there for too long, is like leaving milk outside the fridge, it'll eventually rot. Opportunities must be seized, and risks taken, in a calculated way I guess but like Clint Eastwood said, "If you want a guarantee, just buy a toaster."

At the end I can say that this journey took a whole different route than the one I had planned out. For me it went from a discussion, to analyzing and articulating which ended up with adding perspective which was an element of surprise on its own!

Being myself usually I'd accept things I agree with, things that could relate to my mindset, or something I feel is speaking to me on the same level. To be honest when I decided to do this Q&A, I expected most of what was going to be said to fall into place according to the way I perceive things. Then I was hit with reality. Which is that nothing actually did, nothing spoke to my level, or related to my mindset. This triggered me to be honest, because why? I wanted easier discussions that I would get and relate to, to agree with and discuss.

When this almost never happened, it triggered me. Then when the pistol shot, the bullet came out saying "PERSPECTIVE". So, I decide if nothing is going to make sense to me, I'll make sense out of it. Which led to my analysis, then writing this piece, but mostly giving me an understanding of the true meaning of the word perspective. This bullet of perspective made me understand how to look at things from all the angles possible, not just the one I am pointed at. Therefore, I would like to thank everyone I asked who didn't speak on my level and thank that pistol that led to all of this.

Overall, it was a moment of widening my scope and adding perspective, of not simply collecting answers, but understanding a few things behind the answers. However, I can't deny that I had fun sticking my chopsticks into everyone else's sushi, even though I had no idea what the hell was in their sushi rolls. But even though eating all this sushi made me full for the time, I never lose my appetite. So, like Porky Pig says, "That's all folks!" (But just for now.)

Self-Discrimination and Falafel

So, I am sitting there scrolling through TikTok, Instagram or even Facebook and I am watching a set of different videos and skits. Many of them are titled with "Every Egyptian household", "Tell me you're a Latina without telling me you're Latina", "As the older child you must have…", "Growing up in a black household", and many more things of the same idea. Like, for example, a few of the videos I've watched are about the "OlDeR SibLinG" and how they are supposed to be tough, they don't cry, they watch out for their siblings, they are overprotective, they skip on their own feelings to look out for their siblings' feelings, they do the "mom" roles, and many more. Which could make sense on a few levels. As a twenty-something Egyptian older sibling I watch all this content, relate to some and laugh about others, yet what I began seeing in these videos are capillaries that contribute to building and creating a form of an identity crisis.

These videos are just one way to an identity crisis, they are one of many things that identity crisis resides within all around us, but if we look clearly, we see social roles that supposedly shape every ounce of our existence.

All this social media content (videos as an example), roles, pressures, sense of belonging and many more, are nothing but a portrayal of how we are expected to act based on our background, age, nationality, ethnicity, even birth order, our family, friends' group, and other self-defining elements. Which leads to the fact that not acting in a specific way or having a set of specific preferences that comply with such content directly leads to a personal attack by one's self on one's sense of belonging. It's not how people expect us to act, it's more about how we expect ourselves to act, after we categorize ourselves as a set of labels, and to not fall in status in any of the things I have mentioned above.

One way to look at it are these videos and skits. After watching them you begin feeling "okay this makes sense", then you begin observing your surrounding in a way that would confirm such perceptions of the thing that was discussed in the video. After such observations we tend to find that people do act in a certain way, because our brain becomes wired to observe what we are looking for. Not saying that it's uncommon and everyone is just delusional; it's there and widespread yet we tend to become laser focused when it's what we are looking for. Then begins the comparison where one starts looking at how they act and their preference in this category vs. all the "observed" surrounding. After that a person begins self-discriminating upon themselves because they don't seem to fall in the category.

It begins with comparing, leading questioning, ending up with a feeling of discrimination upon our OWN SELVES. That is caused by thoughts of non-belonging, where not acting in a specific way or liking specific things means that we are less of this or less of that, because we were bound to believe that due to what we have been exposed to. These videos are just one way or simply an example of how the content we are exposed to can lead to such feeling.

Another way to look at it could be my "Hot Tameya" theory. "Tameya" is the Egyptian version of Falafel. The difference between them is that in Egypt we use Fava beans to make the dough of the Falafel instead of chickpeas or "hummus". For those who are interested to know what they are, "Tameya" is made from Fava beans blended with a set of different greens and spices to create a green dough, that is later fried and consumed mainly as breakfast. "Tameya" is usually considered as Egyptian street food and is considered as one of the staple Egyptian breakfast foods.

So, to get back to the theory. I hate "Tameya", it gives me heartburn, it's very salty for my taste, and the flavor itself I consider as mediocre. But because I am Egyptian from an extremely Egyptian background, hot "Tameya" for breakfast is considered a big deal! Even if I am with my family, I am at work, when I was in college, when it was announced that hot "Tameya" was present everyone would rally for breakfast. It's like someone said the two magic words, and everyone fell under the spell. It's the highlight of any Egyptian's morning, sometimes if it was really hot and goooooooddd people would tell the story of the great "Tameya" they had for breakfast to their friends and family. Like how many times have I listened to "Oh my god, today I had some awesome 'Tameya' for breakfast, I totally recommend the place, no way I am eating anything else today!" In this moment I stand there speechless wondering if it's more proper to say "OH CONGRATS!" Or just "Okay, good for you" after this highly expressive breakfast story. Yet I usually end up with a simple,

"That' awesome next time just count me in!" (As a joke of course, praying they never do.)

All of this makes me begin to compare myself of course. Why don't I like it? Why is it such a big deal for everybody else and not me? Next up I begin questioning. Why don't I share this acquired Egyptian taste with everyone, thinking this does not match my very Egyptian background. Lastly, discriminating upon my own personal preference, that I must love "Tameya" (even though I don't), it's not right that I don't (even though it's not illegal not to).

It ended up with me spending years convincing myself that not only I like it but that I love it. Regardless of how much I didn't vibe with its taste, texture nor flavor, nor my digestive tract because it was always automatic HEARTBURN with "Tameya"!

After all of that I would still have it throughout the years, convinced that I enjoy it. Even the few times I said I don't feel like having any or that I don't really like it no one would judge me or even care that I did not want any. The only person who was judging me was ME! Feeling that this must not be the case,

I was discriminating against my own self to fit in with my background, even though my own background was not bothered by my personal preference. My example is a "to scale" version of many things or the real deal, even though it's not too small because it wasn't worth all the uncomfortable breakfast moments.

Examples like my Falafel story (alongside many things), social media content and several other things can make us question our whole belonging, which leads to the "identity crisis". Where one tends to feel that they don't fall in a certain definitive criterion which is status affecting to anything they belong to. It could also be because we feel that not falling into such criteria would make us left out, or disappoint others we care about. Therefore we tend not to complement ourselves and preference just to avoid such events from happening, which leads to an "I D E N T I T Y C R I S I S."

Just to keep things clear the identity crisis is basically when a person is not able to fully identify themselves: it is the "Who am I?" or "What defines me?" question. It's when a person is confused about who they are, where they belong, their likes and dislikes, their beliefs even their purpose in life in general it could be identified as confusion of what shapes them.

The identity crisis has been studied and analyzed by many. One of these analyses is provided by the German American psychologist Erik Erikson, in his book *Identity, Youth and Crisis* where he presents his psychosocial analysis.

This psychosocial analysis could be compared to Freud's psychosexual analysis. The difference is Freud discusses phases of sexual development, while Erikson discusses the phases of social and identity development.

In his psychosocial analysis Erikson discuss the stages of identity formation in eight stages. Each stage falls under a certain age or phase, in this analysis each age group is analyzed from birth to death. Each phase mentioned by Erikson is an area where a part of each human being's identity is formed. Erikson puts this as a dispute between two things, which is settled by a question a human begins finding an answer to throughout this phase of their life, through a set of events that take place mentioned as the "major events" of this phase.

We can look at adolescence as an example. Adolescence is mainly focused between forming an identity vs. role confusion, the main questions are 'Who am I?' and 'Where am I going?' and the major events are identity-shaping experiences (like an occupational internship for example where a person explores a specific field) and/or social relationships constructed and/or developed. Therefore, the human during adolescence begins forming their identity by thinking who they are, where they are going, where they fit in. In this part of the person's life the person begins building a sense of self. They begin to find who they are between themselves and other people, through building new relationships and having experiences. Being able to identify identity leading to fidelity, which means faithfulness to one's self and beliefs. When a person is not faithful nor accepting to themselves during this period this leads to role confusion when the person does not have a clear stance on identity.

Each age period has its own dispute, question, events, and virtue/outcome, which defines its role in identity formation according to Erikson in his psychosexual analysis, shown in the following table:

Stage	Dispute	Questions	Events	Virtue/ outcome
Infancy 0–18 months	Trust vs. Mistrust	Is my world safe?	Feeding Comfort	Hope
Early Childhood 2–3 years	Autonomy vs. Shame and Doubt	Can I do things myself?	Using the toilet Dressing	Will
Preschool 3–5 years	Initiative vs. Guilt	Am I Good? Am I Bad?	Exploration of different items and activity Playing	Purpose

School age 6–11 years	Industry vs. Inferiority	How can I be good?	Serious activity School	Confidence
Adolescences 12–18 years	Identity vs. Role Confusion	Who am I? Where is my life headed?	Personal choices Social relationships	Fidelity
Young Adult 19–40 years	Intimacy vs. Isolation	Am I wanted? Am I loved?	Intimate relationships	Love
Middle Adult 40–65 years	Generativity vs. Stagnation	Will I provide something of value?	Work and parenthood	Care
Maturity 65 up to death	Ego vs. Despair	Have I lived a full/ fulfilling life?	Reflection	Wisdom

James Marcia then builds on Erikson's Theory of Identity, forming his Theory of Identity Development in Adolescence. Marcia states that for one to achieve identity, they must construct preferences based on experiences and commit to such preferences to achieve identity. Marcia creates four categories for this notion:

    1- Identity achievement

    When a person in adolescence engages in experiences and then commits to his identity based on conclusions of those experiences. A simple way of explaining is sports. So, let's say a person is a basketball player and on weekends they engage in some tennis. The person found out this about themselves because they tried ten other sports which they didn't like as much and found themselves to prefer basketball and tennis. Then they seemed to enjoy playing those two sports, therefore basketball and tennis construct a part of their identity.

2- Identity Foreclosure

When a person does not engage in any identity defining experiences, and accept a given to become an identity-constructing element without exploring others. Using the same sports example, could be a person who is raised between basketball players. Therefore, accepting and becoming a basketball player by default, without exploring any other sport, and defining themselves as a basketball player.

3- Identity Moratorium

When a person engages in different experiences yet does not seem to commit to any of the conclusions they gain from such experience. In a simple way it could be that person tries twenty different sports yet does not seem to engage in any specific sports, yet engages in many of them generally, even if they seemed to prefer basketball over others.

4- Identity Confusion (which is mentioned by Erikson)

The state when a person does not engage in any experiences, and doesn't commit to anything in return, whether based on experience or not. It's like when a person doesn't try any sports, doesn't engage in any, and has no idea what sport they prefer.

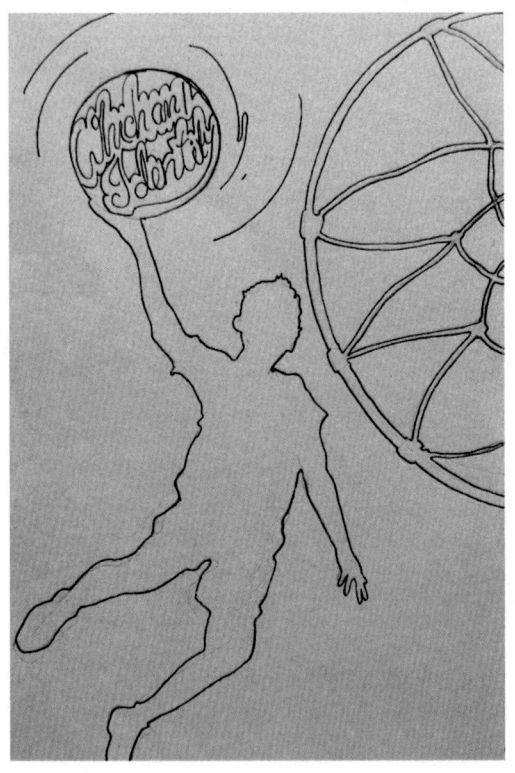

What Marcia and Erikson argue is a whole world of self-exploration and identity formation based on many elements. Yet when it comes to self-discrimination it is more focused on the area of adolescence by Erikson which is touched upon by Marcia. Which I believe goes beyond adolescence. As life is filled with different experiences that are identity defining throughout the human's life course, therefore, a person must form a conclusion of every experience they undergo regardless of if it's simple like food or sport, or deeper like social relationships, career choices, hobbies, and others. Therefore, I believe that with every experience we undergo throughout our lives it can be a change or better to say a "development" to our identity, because identity is not set in stone, maybe the basis is, yet the rest can always be developed, changed, and upgraded (and between us how do you think wise people are made? It's just a matter of continuous concluding and improvement).

One thing that can be hard to accept is choosing your own preferences over your sense of belonging. Because refusing something of one's own belonging is much harder than to accept what you actually prefer. Due to a decreased sense of belonging, fear of not being accepted, judgment or not fitting in!

Trying to like, accept, comply with what you don't and thinking it would affect your belonging or status you naturally acquire, is simply a ticking identity crisis bomb, because it leads to questioning the whole sense of belonging which defines the basics I mentioned above, leading to Marcia's idea of Identity Moratorium, where a person is unable to commit to their own experiences and conclusions.

The Falafel story could be a way to explain how self-discrimination of one's experience could lead to an identity crisis. If me trying Falafel is my way of experiencing, then not committing to my preference that I established based on the experience is BOOM an identity crisis. Due to thinking of how I am not "Egyptian" enough, because I want a bagel for breakfast more than "Tameya".

What I am trying to say is, if one tries something and likes it more than something they supposedly 'belong to' and does not accept their preference, they are going against their own unique identity. Which could lead to more "Who am I?" questions or the feeling of being undeserving of nationality or ethnicity. Therefore, experiencing something and creating a standing on it is actually a power not everyone has.

Standing there and being able to say yes or no based on

personal preference is a SUPER POWER, that could only be diminished by a fake sense of belonging.

So regardless of if it's based on a video, external pressure, or simply just comparison, a rising notion I have been noticing with all the interconnectedness of the world, is self-discrimination.

Everyday new world orders are shaped with increased accessibility and interconnectedness. It's like the world we live in isn't big enough after it became all wired and connected, so the human race has no other option but to plan to move to Mars (lol).

Today's world is privileged with interconnectedness (and cursed more or less), experiences are now easier. We live in a world where everything is easy, close, and extremely accessible (touch of a button accessible). Therefore, easier access is directly proportionate to higher exposure.

According to Marcia, engaging in experiences and committing to our preference that we concluded upon them, is a premise for identity formation. Therefore, having easier access to such experiences is a privilege, that can be demolished by being unable to commit to them, because one's discrimination upon themselves. Which is a road that leads to an identity crisis.

So, trying and seeing different things that you may like more than your own is what makes you unique, it's an indicator that you are you and you are part of the modern world. So don't discriminate upon yourself to feel more fitting, because personal preferences are no takeaway from your background, ethnicity, or belongingness. One fighting their own preferences and not committing to their "experience-based preference" is just a key to an identity crisis. Sometimes it's the smaller things like the bigger, and never forget that nothing is too small nor too big.

Yet there is only a fine line between being true to one's self and deviation. Jumping this line turns your way to rooting your identity to a taboo. So a person must keep themselves true to their beliefs, like truth to preferences.

Because, as mentioned by Marcia, the notion of Identity Foreclosure is also a premise of identity formation. A person accepting a set of beliefs and values (like morals or religions) is also a main part in identity formation.

There are a set of examples of such conformation:

1- The Social Contract, introduced by Rousseau in his book *The Social Contract*. Where he states that people conform to the society, they live in by accepting its laws and norms, giving it the ability to act. This is a way of conformation to a doctrine of the society, someone could not commit theft even if it is not against one's belief, yet it's against the society therefore it's not acceptable. Therefore the person does not commit such theft not only as it goes against one's own morals, but against the state's morals the person has conformed to by being part of it. Therefore, as stated by Rousseau, the Social Contract is a metaphorical contract constructed between the state and the people to maintain order of the state and general well-being, this is an example of basic conformation.

2- Argument of Virtue, introduced by Aristotle. Where a man should have traits and values that makes them virtuous. Virtuous means that a human has traits that make them the best being they could be or in simpler words "a good person". Aristotle has presented a set of traits which are Prudence, Justice, Temperance and Courage. These are a set of essential virtue according to Aristotle. However, the main concept of virtue according to Aristotle is finding the balances between two vices (extremes). Where is the middle of both of those vices is the 'virtue', courage as an example is the middle of between being cowardly and reckless, therefore virtue is in courage. So, it was essential for people to find balance of certain traits in order to achieve virtue.

Some may conform with Aristotle's philosophies and try to practice these traits that would make them a "virtuous" being (a good person). Therefore, they have exercised Identity Foreclosure in which a person has chosen and confirmed such personality conduction technique in order to achieve specific traits (finding balance, to gain specific characteristics) in order to form their identity, without any actual experience to confirm.

3- Religion. Having a set of beliefs and following a certain religion constructs a great part of an identity, as it is a conformation to a set of beliefs, a whole doctrine. Therefore, one must find a doctrine to use as a compass through identity-constructing experiences. A religion provides certain practices and beliefs, therefore accepting and following a certain religion is conformation to the beliefs and practices. Which is tends to become a code of conduct in certain situations.

I believe that a person's identity must be constructed through experiences and foreclosure. Whereas accepting beliefs and building on them is a paved way for identity formation.

Therefore, when a person is accepting of a set beliefs, and builds their preferences on them without any self-discrimination they are bound to find their best balance of their own unique identity. That is fitting, accepting, and is made up of all the acquired elements.

I am not saying that it's an easy thing to establish, yet as written in "The Unabridged Journals of Sylvia Plath", Sylvia Plath once said, "It's hell of a responsibility to be yourself. It's much easier to be somebody else."

Yet, it's the best and lightest way to go through a heavy life.

So, at the end I hope no one must work to belong somewhere, and I hope if we need to work to belong somewhere, I hope this somewhere is one's self, because as Agesilaus (King of Sparta) once said, "It's not the land that honors the man, it's the man that honors the land." Which for me it means that we create the place we belong to, not the place that defines us. This, my friends, is not only applicable to land, but to everything that contributes into shaping a human being's identity. Because it's us who shape our surrounding, not only do our surroundings shape us!

Invisible Stamp

We are many things in this world, many things to many people. Yet there is always that pungent thing about each one's personality that shapes a chunky part of who they are, it's usually not a pretty word, nor is it a compliment. It's usually some sort of funky adjective that won't sweep you off your feet yet won't bother you as well (it's about perception I guess) adjectives like intimidating, selfless, sneaky, crazy, rebellious, slow and that sort of thing. They are not necessarily bad, like I said (regardless that the words themselves aren't pretty), it's just that each word is a symbol to the overriding tweak in someone's persona, and for me tweaks are never described in pretty words.

Each of these "adjectives" are an identity status that carry more within them, and represent a few things, and say something about how a person is projected. Throughout this piece I'll call these "adjectives" Invisible Stamps.

I think some of us could recognize theirs just by reading the intro and before actually going deep into the piece, while others may not. Yet through digging deeper the idea begins to formulate itself, and the concept itself can be deduced easier.

There is a fraction of us I must mention though, the people who actually get bluntly told their Invisible Stamp from people in their surroundings, rooting from their closest dearest circle, they may recognize it or not, but they actually hear it out loud as bluntly as "Dude you are so…"

Regardless of any of the ways mentioned we simply get to

experience it in our surrounding, regardless of being bluntly told the stamp or not. Experience rooting from how we are treated, addressed, and in some way allocated. For example, let's take an actress who always plays the role of a yogi in her movies, no one tells her "OMG, you look like such a yogi", but most of the roles she's given shows that she gives off yogi vibes. There's something about her that makes her a perfect fit as a yogi, regardless of if she actually is. This is a simple example of what I mean by allocated, it's the way we are positioned because the perception of it is most fitting.

Again, I say, this is not being treated badly, it's just like a cookie cutter that ends up shaping a person's silhouette in the lives of people that surround them like the cutter shapes the dough into the cookie.

Okay so I briefed the idea, now allow me to bring my Frankenstein monster to life by making it personal!

So at some point in life, I was on a family trip in Vienna. Me and my mom are strolling through some of the most beautiful gardens I've ever seen and then someone suddenly played some music, I guess, (specifically I think it was a Mozart, and regarding the fact I was Vienna, it was a little cliché.) and involuntarily I find myself dancing. (I just love music so much!) This follows up with a quick but important conversation with my mom.

I'll recreate my conversation with my G (aka mom), so after I began to dance:

G: Ahahhahah what are you doing?

Me: Music is fireeee.

G: *in a laughing, nothing bad intended yet not joking tone* You are out of your mind, you know you're crazy rightt?

I laughed for a moment (giving a little vibe of disregard) then said: Come dance with me!

Disregarding my disregard in the moment itself, I cannot deny that this was a moment of ignition. Which meant that from this moment onwards my craziness became a little bit more visible to me, or I began noticing it much clearer.

To follow up. I was there talking to one of my dearest and most trusted friends, and we are having this heated conversation about friends, life, and philosophies. Discussing some problems we had with other people, then adding the Cajun spice by concluding some annotations from our encounters, problems, conversation, and discussions. Formulating ideas of our own, which we see as pretty valuable (lol). Then throughout this convo I got too comfortable and shot a very frank unfiltered opinion.

(Off topic: I am a person who believes in filtering words just to make what I am trying to say in the best shape possible. Makes it easier for me to speak my mind and being accepted most of the time I do so, and on lucky days even convincing. I don't change them I just carve them). So back to my story. My friend who I love very badly stopped, smiled and with the same laughing, no bad intended yet not joke tone said, "Aya you are crazy." This time I happily linked up quickly and it did not catch me with the same amount of surprise it did with my mom, and I said "Maybe! But why?"

Then I got a reply that drove me LITERALLY crazy, which simply was "I don't know, you just are." At this point I realized that I need answers; those are two prominent people in my life, and this is beyond unsatisfactory.

At this point I had two important self-discovery questions, which are the following:

1- Am I actually crazy?
2- If yes, why?

So, a person like me cherishes their closed, trusted circle very much, I associate with them, depend on them, think through them and with them, and most of all I love them so much it hurts.

Which means that they were my first resort when I was looking for answers. Therefore, I went around and asked pretty much all of them (which by this point you must have found out that I have no problem with calling someone up just because I have an existential question, which I personally categorize as extremely urgent even if the person I am calling doesn't). So, with no intro provided I lead the conversation with "Do you think I am crazy?" and I will not lie to you, pretty much no one said no. Everyone said yes too quickly. I was amazed, some even said it with a tone of "How are you just realizing that now?" Like I must be joking. The follow up question by default was, "Why though?" Which was not met with the same speedy answers. Obviously, this was the harder question, because when I asked this one everyone just stuttered and paused.

One of my dear beloveds told me it's because I am different, that they've never met or will meet anyone like me again. This person told me that they can meet many people like them and like a few of their friends, but I was just too different to be found again.

You know guys till this point I never thought I would have this much trouble with identifying if something is actually good or bad, was it an embrace or a disgrace. This was an extreme point of personal paradox for me, but you know what they say, the show must go on.

Another answer to my question was, "You are one of the most unexpected people I've ever met! Aya, you could be on your way to a place, and we'd randomly find out you took a U-turn and ended in someplace else, you are just too unexpected to be sane." This one was so me I couldn't disagree, or actually I agreed too much I sort of liked the explanation. It was an 'explanation comfort zone'.

I'll give you a final one just to keep you guys in the loop, and to show you how many definitions "crazy" can hold. One of the people I asked told me that I am the human version of a rollercoaster, that I am super inconsistent, it's crazy. So, I simply replied that I am not hot n cold at all; I am emotionally stable toward many things if not all. They said not like that but it's more like a push n pull. "You push yourself too far in and then you pull yourself out, and then sometimes you push in again one time or a few." Then she provided an explanation which I won't share just to keep a personal element for the next book (lol).

See all these different explanations for one adjective. It was all a matter of expression, but for everyone I gave the same vibe, like they received the same sense of craziness from me.

Another very noticeable aspect was how they all felt it, believed it, yet loved it about me. It was a form of unconditional love and acceptance that I am always thankful I got to experience. So even though I was considered crazy I was accepted, adored, and celebrated for all of my craziness.

My mom once told me, "I think you've been called crazy too much; it doesn't alert nor bother you any more." You guys can call me crazy if you want too, but I can see how proud she was while she was telling me this. Like what she's saying is, you grew some thick skin, or you are now comfortable enough with who you are and unapologetically embracing it. I guess the pride is also because of how much she grew to love this part about me, it is unique and definitive

So even though I am identified as a crazy person, (which all great people are) I am happily enjoying it, it's became a part of my uniqueness (which I strongly enjoy).

A less personal story is the story of one of my favorite people of all time, the amazing Frida Kahlo (a quick fun fact about me is that I am obsessed with Frida in terms of work, life, and personality. For me she is not only an artist, she is a work of art).

To anyone who doesn't know who Frida Kahlo is, this is a quick Frida 101.

Frida Kahlo is a Mexican painter (her work is mainly focused on surrealism, cubism, and the modern art movement). Frida resided on planet earth from 1907—1954 (and was a Cancer to whoever is interested). Frida was a Mexican originating from the city Coyoacan and did reside in Mexico for most of her life.

Frida's work is known for being personal, as her paintings mainly focus on her painful life experiences, one of her famous quotes is: "My paintings carry with it the message of pain." She also said, "I paint myself because I am so often alone, and I am the subject I know best." It's dark but amazing (I highly recommend navigating her work).

Here is a quick list of work by Frida Kahlo:
1- The two Fridas — 1939.
2- Henry Ford Hospital — 1932.
3- The Broken Column — 1944.
4- Self Portrait with Bonito — 1941.

5- Diego and I — 1949.

Frida was married, on and off, to the famous muralist Diego Rivera. Frida and Diego were communists, and engaged in political activity during their lives, and were part of the communist movement.

JOURNAL ENTRY

Okay so it has been a whileeee since I sat down and actually got any writing done. Let me tell you why!

I got a procedure done in my teeth which ended up with me getting a tooth extraction, which supposedly went well. Then a few days later I woke up and I am seeing things in fours, threes, and any quantity except one, then a sudden squint appears in my left eye (the literal meaning of a bad eye day). So, imagine with me I was perfectly fine then suddenly blurry vision and a shifted eye (took me a moment to comprehend), so I began checking in with doctors (and of course not writing BTW missed you).

Turns out the anesthesia I got for my tooth procedure was toxic and got me a nerve infection, so I am currently doing life one eye at a time till it goes back to normal.

Moral of the story is anything could happen, good more than bad of course, we just must make something out of it. That's why I am currently writing with an eye patch.

So, regardless of my Journal Entry and back to what I was saying. So, I am sitting reading a biography about Frida and I cannot help but find a reoccurring trend, and as I focus more it turns to be an Invisible Stamp that seems to have lived with her, then lived on to shape her silhouette in the minds of people that learn about her or even portray her till the current day. This is that Frida was a "Rebel". Frida was an outgoing person who was known to have played by her own rules and followed none but her own self. Therefore, she did not mainly confide with all the pre-existing rules, which means she broke some of the existing rules and created a set of others for herself.

This led to her portrayal as a "Rebel".

Frida's whole life screamed rebellion, yet many famous prominent moments of Frida's life could be used as an example of what led to the pungency of the rebellious side. Each of these moments have screamed rebellion; however, each moment of those was simply a moment of self-expression.

You know, for me, this raises a question. The question is:

If by expressing myself I go against the rule, does this make the rule weaker, or does it just make me different and the rule lives untouched?

So back to Frida, and in a way, her aesthetic. How Frida looked and chose to present herself is one of the loudest examples that could be looked at when examining this 'Rebellious' stamp. Frida is known for her famous uni-brow which became a trademark for Frida's look till the current day (let's be honest if you decide to dress as Frida for Halloween, you can't do it with no uni-brow). She also kept a mustache which wasn't usual as well. This for Frida was a form of expression, it was a way to express her identity and artistic style, regardless of the idea that women should not keep their mustache and uni-brow that highly visible. For women facial hair was usually supposed to be tamed or removed. Yet for Frida she chose to express her personal style, artistic style, and uniqueness through leaving this facial hair, this mustache, this uni-brow, even though she was maybe "rebelling" against the feminine rules.

There's also the famous family portrait where Frida is in a suit. This was highlighted in the movie Frida issued in 2002 (I highly recommend) where she supposedly enters the room where the family picture is being taken with a suit as a surprise, in a moment where she was supposed to be in a dress (nicely and femininely dressed) for the family picture. Frida was about nineteen in the picture.

This was another act of expression by Frida where she expressed herself for herself. I don't think she thought anyone else would see this very personal family picture, so I guess this excludes the fact of her trying to prove a point or take a stance, and maybe if she did it was an act of self-expression of one's self with no further intention. In my opinion I always perceive this act as her saying that nothing is set in stone, that women can wear a suit, that suits aren't for men, or that maybe she was just projecting her masculine side, which for Frida didn't have to be tamed.

Politics was another roar that shaped Frida Kahlo's life. Frida was a communist who was married to a communist. They were also Trotskyists. Which explains why, during the inter-war era, she and Diego kept Leon Trotsky at Frida's home (the blue house) to protect him from assassination attempts directed at him from the USSR.

Quick recap, who was Leon Trotsky?

He was a Russian-Ukrainian Marxist and Political Activist. Trotsky had a vital role in leading the Red Army, and the victory of the Bolshevik Revolution. Trotsky was part of the movement yet was then expelled after Stalin conciliated power after the death of Vladimir Lenin, the leader of the Revolution. As Trotsky did not agree with Stalin's rule. Which led to his expulsion, and assassination attempts.

At the time Leon Trotsky was expelled from the USSR, his first resort the Norwegian government refused to grant him asylum. Therefore, Diego who was a Trotskyist interceded with the Mexican President and permitted him asylum in Mexico at the time.

Diego offered to grant him protection and hospitality in his wife's home, Frida agreed upon Diego's wishes and accepted him in her blue house where her father resided granting him asylum after his expulsion from the USSR.

Frida believed in communism; she was a hard-core communist. Frida believed in Trotsky and his ideology and believed that he was worthy of protection. But most of all Frida believed in Diego Rivera (whom she wrote for him in one of her letters to him "I love you more than my own skin"). Therefore, she agreed to shelter Trotsky with Diego.

For some people this act is portrayed as a duty toward personal beliefs, for many others this a rebellious and dangerous act regarding the position of Mexico during the Second World War in aiding the USA which was the enemy of the USSR. Alongside the fact that the USSR was attempting to assassinate Trotsky, which is enough danger on its own. Yet she stuck to her beliefs and did something not many would have done. Again, Frida here wasn't rebelling, she was fulfilling an act of duty.

Frida is also known to have had an affair with Leon Trotsky whom she gave a self-portrait titled, "Her self-portrait dedicated to Leon Trotsky" for his birthday. This affair was built on the fascination Frida had with the revolutionary and his charisma and how Trotsky was fascinated by Frida as a person and an artist.

Throughout her life Frida was known to have had multiple affairs with multiple (famous) figures throughout her life while she was married and while she wasn't. It was a peculiar nature for a marriage, yet this was how her relationship and marriage with Diego was shaped. Frida and Diego's marriage was on and off, yet when Frida died, Diego and Frida were married. This is another indication of rebellion, as the nature of her marriage and relationship with Rivera was another "rebellious" element in its nature.

Frida's work on its own played by its own rules because it was a reflection of her own self and her life. Frida's work portrays her pain, her life, how she changed and grew, how she expressed herself, it was Frida's work that was her loudest expression for her "rebellion".

For me, as painful as Frida's life was, I can only imagine her tears on canvas as if she only cried in paint. In my head I could never see her crying in person, she reflected her pain too boldly in her work that for me a few drops of paint on canvas spoke louder than actual tears. Like Frida said about her work "My paintings carry with it the message of pain."

All of Frida's life could be deduced from her work, her work was loud and bold. Yet I cannot speak of her work without touching base with her life itself. Frida's life and work are one soul in two bodies.

So, her work was no more than expression of her own self, like Frida said about her work "My paintings are the frankest expression of myself, without taking into consideration either judgments or prejudices of anyone". Frida's art speaks to many, yet it's no rebellion; it's simply her.

One example could be her painting "My Dress Hanging There", which was one of the few that aren't self-portraits, yet it was still a representation of her. At this part of her life, Frida went with Diego to New York City where he had a work offer.

This painting was how she portrayed herself (the dress) around all the madness of New York city, and how it was too much for her at the time, and how SHE perceived the city. But most of all it was a portrayal of how she saw her culture, and how it was different and unfitting with "Gringolandia".

Frida and Diego reached a few dark places in their relationship, and this painting was created during one of them. Therefore, Frida felt as if she's "Hanging There" in New York city, where she went with her husband Diego, and ended up odd and alone, around all of the madness.

I can agree that this is rebellion. Frida in her life had no rules but her own which is the meaning of rebellion. Yet as I learn more about her, I find Frida wasn't rebelling against anything, she was simply expressing and identifying herself, which stamped her as a "Rebel".

And to end this Frida mini-biography I'll give you one last quote:

"It's not worthwhile to leave this world without having had a little fun in life".

JOURNAL ENTRY

So, the squint in my eye is getting a lot better and I am back to playing my keyboard like a violin (the clicking itself is just music to my ears, always). I took off the eye patch, thank God, and I am getting my vision back gradually. I had to deal with extreme sarcasm and extreme sympathy every day because this is life with an eye patch on, but what choice did I have?

Regardless it's always good to be back two eyes at a time.

Moral of the story is sometimes sarcasm could be a lot better to hear than sympathy. I just realized too much sympathy is like too many cheeseburgers, it just makes me feel sluggish.

Back to stamping!

I'll give you guys another quick example of an Invisible Stamp. This time it's more personal than Frida, but still less personal than my own experience, it's the story of one of my friends.

This friend was always labeled as slow. Like when we'd talk about this person, we'd always say they're slow, a slow taker, slow in making decisions, slow in getting jokes, slow getting ready, etc.

Let me tell you it is to the extent that when this person just begins to tell us a story we instantly shift to bored, because it's automatic this person is slow, even though we did not give them a chance to start talking, and that they may actually not be slow. Like it's default, when they decide to tell a story we are automatically bored.

Sometimes it gets as far as that because they are slow, we give them a heads up that we aren't planning to listen for long (as a joke of course, and it is a joke). So, it becomes a default that whenever this person decides to speak, before they even attempt it it's always going to be a slow story (even though it's very normal paced). But because they were stamped as slow, it became something that most of the time factors in.

This is a story where I, myself, am guilty of invisible stamping.

You know invisible stamps aren't actually bad. There are a few things I love about the concept regardless of anything.

1- The Unconditional love:

This concept is proof that people will love you and accept you with your tweaks. The people around you will listen to your stories even if they are slow as hell, will keep up with you even though you drive them crazy with your ideas and unexpected lifestyle, and that they will accept you even if your way of expression conforms with nothing. It's a cute form of unconditionality. It's like saying, "However you're coded, I'll format myself to be compatible."

2- The people around you are familiar with YOU:

Stamping a person is a way that you say I am familiar with you. It's an "I know you", it's an "I am used to you" and sometimes an "I enjoy you". It's a way that makes a person have their own shape in the lives of others. It's uniqueness, it's when you need someone who is going to do something crazy with you; you know exactly who you are going to call knowing that they will be the perfect fit.

3- Honest:

These stamps are ninety-nine percent true. They originate from our closest surroundings, they aren't something we are usually told, and they aren't that pretty to be fabricated.

So, our stamp is usually something about us that exists in the way we act or the vibe we give, but it's usually not made up if it's deduced from the right place.

4- Indication of being true to one's self:

It's also proof that a person is being themselves. Getting stamped because of who you are is just an indication that you are letting yourself be. Believe me there is no better place to be better than a in an unchained, true version of one's self.

At the end I can't say that the notion for me is something I agree or disagree with. It's just something I noticed and dug a little deep into, till I fell into the pit as usual. Yet as much as I notice it bluntly and boldly, or subtly and quietly: it exists and it's always easier for us to accept ourselves and others for it. Because it has its own beauty of shaping, and like I said I love diversity and for me this is diversity, these are the tweaks that make us who we are.

(I use the word tweaks so much because I romanticize it. Someone's tweaks for me are what I love about them before their traits. It's my way of saying the more globally romanticized "it's the little things").

So, look at your stamps and look at how you stamp everyone around you. Then take a moment to admire your stamp and two moments to admire the one you gave to everyone around you.

Always remember to love the person for their tweaks and their traits before their deeds. It just makes it truer, more resilient, and deeper.

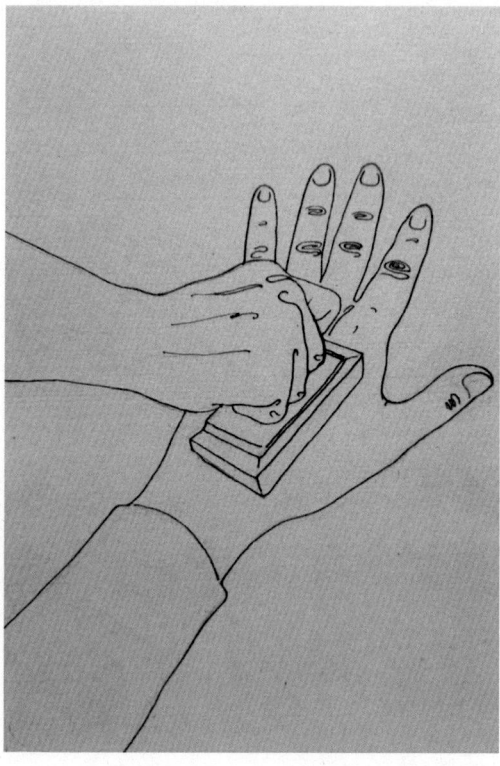

Ending

Yours truly from this moment onwards, with all the love and light there is, Aya.